A Giant First-Start Reader

This easy reader contains only 35 different words,
repeated often to help the young reader develop
word recognition and interest in reading.

Basic word list for *Rainbows and Frogs: A Story About Colors*

a	have	smell
are	here	special
be	how	taste
blue	it	things
can	like	to
color	make	touch
colors	no	what
do	orange	why
does	red	would
feel	say	yellow
feelings	see	yes
green		you

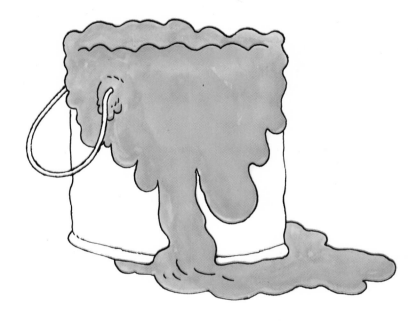

Rainbows and Frogs

A Story About Colors

Written by Joy Kim

Illustrated by Paul Harvey

Troll Associates

Library of Congress Cataloging in Publication Data

Kim, Joy.
    Rainbows and frogs.

    Summary: Introduces the colors red, yellow, green,
orange, and blue and how they make you feel.
    [1. Color] I. Harvey, Paul, 1926-   . II. Title.
PZ7.K5597Rai   [E]   81-4685
ISBN 0-89375-505-2 (lib. bdg.)   AACR2
ISBN 0-89375-506-0 (pbk.)

What are colors?

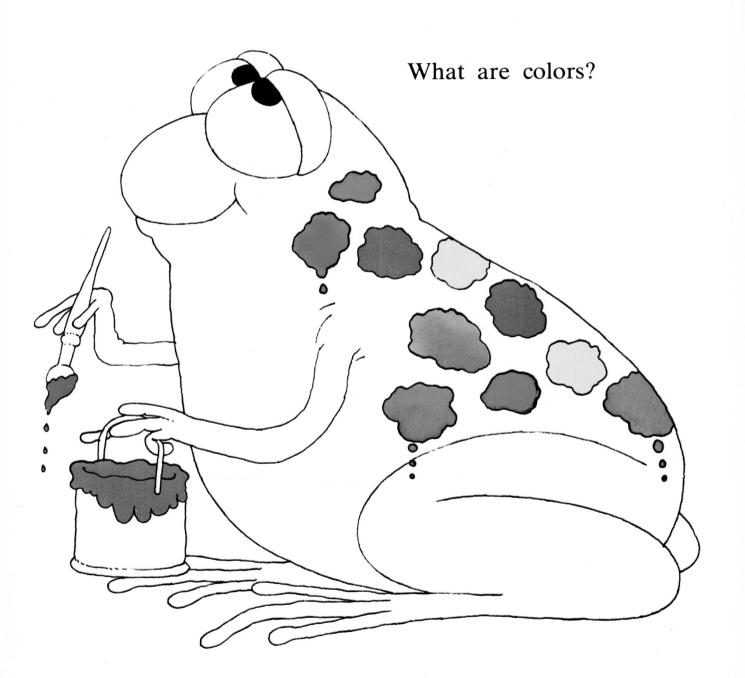

Can you feel it? No.

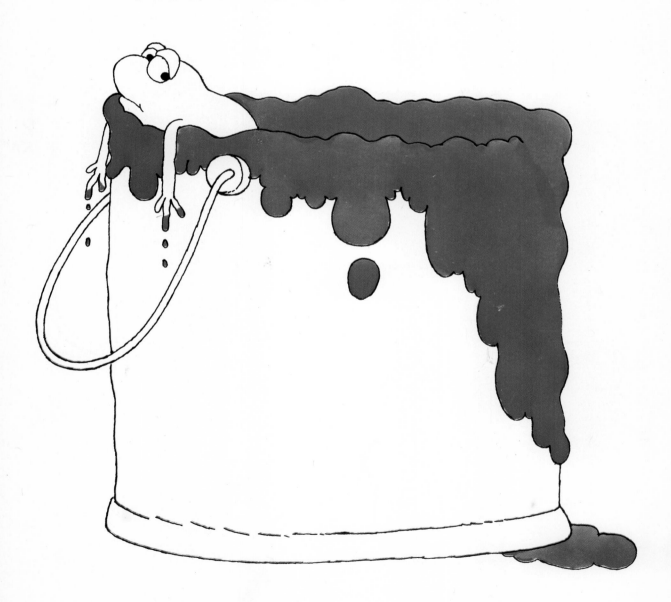

Can you touch it? No.

Can you smell it? No.

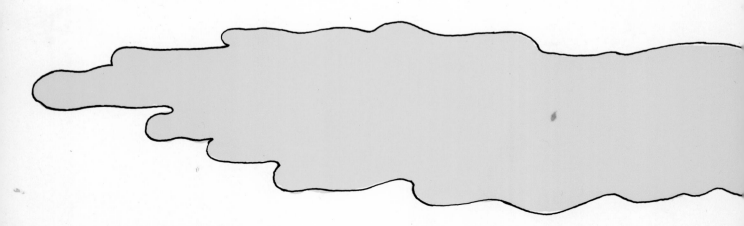

Can you taste it? No.

Can you see it? Yes!

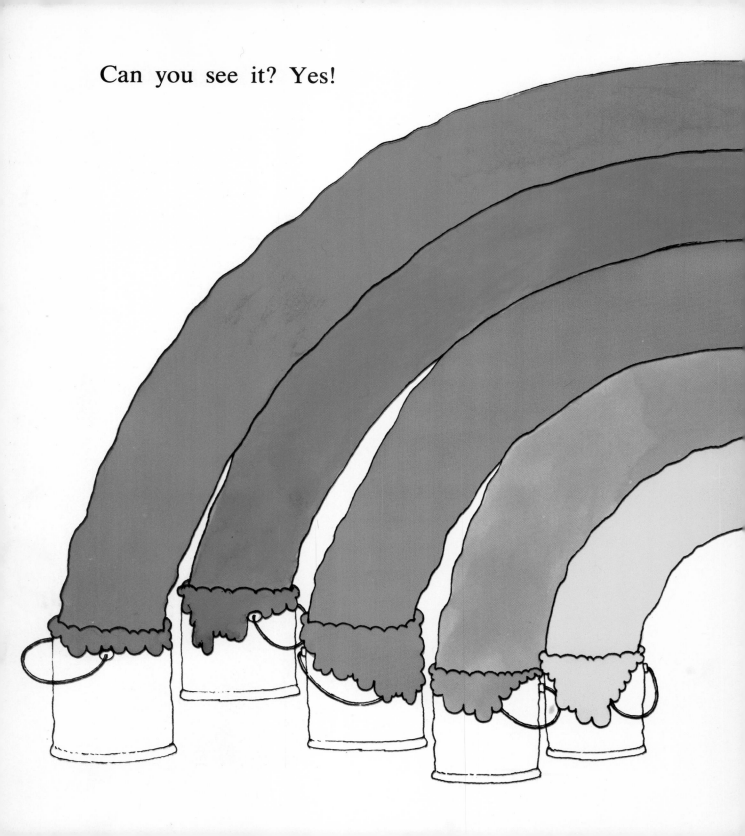

What do you see here?

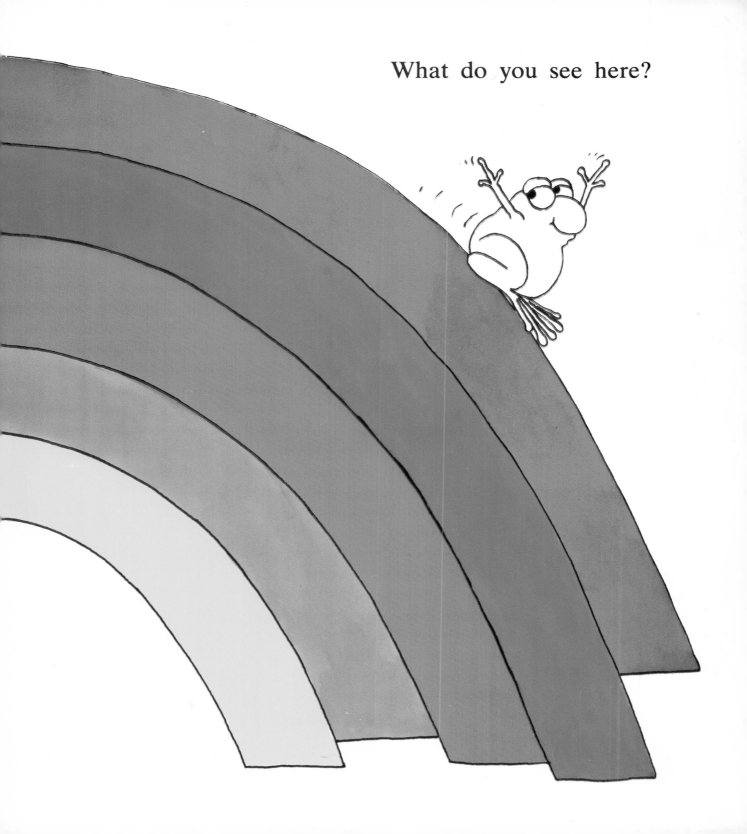

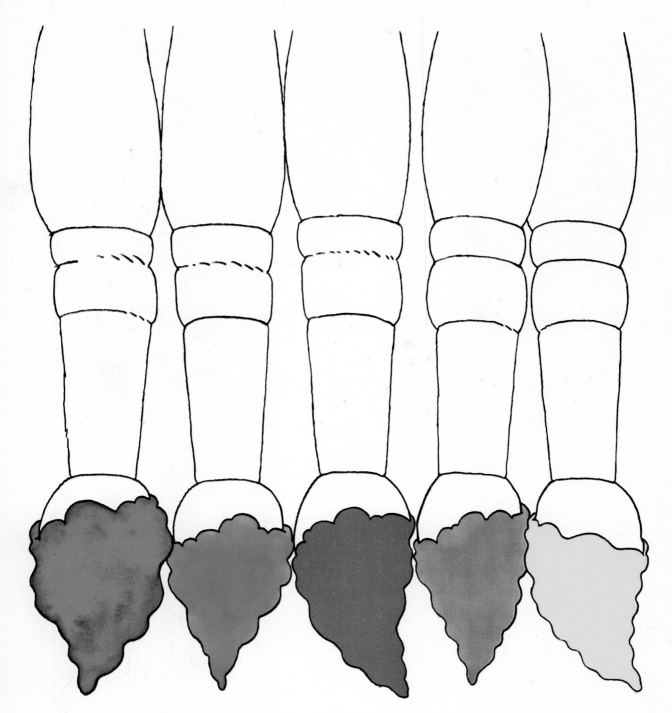

Blue! Green! Red! Orange! Yellow!

Do you like red?

What red things do you like?

Do you like yellow?

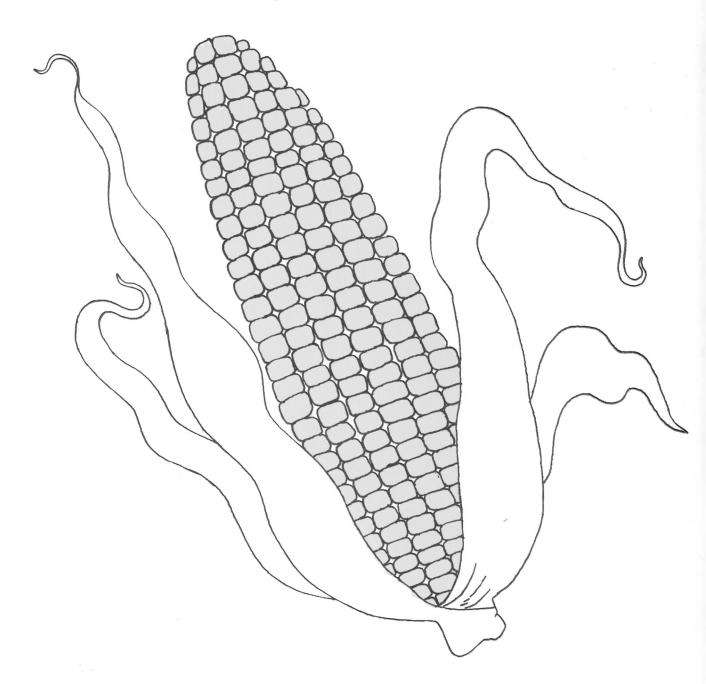

What yellow things do you like?

Do you like green?

What green things do you like?

Do you like orange?

What orange things do you like?

Do you like blue?

What blue things do you like?

Colors are special.

Colors have special feelings.

How does red make you feel?

How does yellow make you feel?

How does green make you feel?

How does blue make you feel?

Would you like to be a color?

What color would you like to be?

Why? Can you say why?